EGIL IS BAFFLED BY GRIEF

NANCY JASPER

PUBLISHERS INFORMATION

EBook Bakery
www.ebookbakery.com

Contact: nancyjasper18@gmail.com

ISBN 978-1-938517-56-3

Cover image: Egil.
From a 17th century manuscript of *Egil's Saga*.

DEDICATION

For Janet

TABLE OF CONTENTS

Preface vii

SECTION I Egil: Variations On A Saga 1

Introduction 2

    Egil 4

    Egil Swims Away From Europe 5

    The Eyebrows 6

    Bear 8

    Egil is Baffled By Grief 9

    Egil is Saved By A Woman 10

    Egil's Mouth 11

    Thorgerd 12

    Arinbjorn 13

    Gunnhild 14

    Egil Faces The Challenges Of Aging 15

SECTION II Snorri: A Lament 17

Introduction 18

    Snorri Learns The World Is Wide 20

    The Old Poems 21

    Edda 22

    Snorri Loses Sleep 23

    Snorri, Cornered 24

    Snorri's Last Words 25

    Egil's Lament 26

SECTION III The Mead Of Poetry 29

Introduction 30

      Commotion 31

      Gunnlod 32

Suggestions For Further Reading 34

Acknowledgments 35

About The Author 37

PREFACE

Wen I was a child, about seven or eight years old, I was fascinated by a children's edition of old Norse stories. I loved the humor and adventure, of course, but they also spoke to a deeper preoccupation. How even the gods might not be all powerful. How you could not bind the Fenris Wolf.

In the 70's and 80's, I discovered Icelandic sagas in Penguin paperback editions. I was moved by these stories and the way these stories were told. I think I was responding to how revenge pulled at these people, how they tried to find the detour out of revenge, how it often would not hold. The stories were violent, but they had a sadness to them, a cost to the violence. And they were funny. Sometimes the humor was dry and understated, sometimes broad.

I loved the complexity of the characters. A short stroke of dialogue or behavior might unsettle your sense of a character you thought you understood. Character was built up in small details, pieces cut uneven. Not much commentary. There was a quietness to it. You had to pay attention.

I did not plan to write a collection of Icelandic poems. A few years ago, I thought I would take a break from writing about my relatives in Jersey City. I wrote a poem about Egil Skallagrimsson, the complicated hero of *Egil's Saga*. I kept on writing, with encouragement from a generous scholar, Professor Christina von Nolcken. She had been open, thank goodness, to receiving an unsolicited poem about Egil.

My hope is that these poems will appeal to readers who have never read a saga and readers who have deep experience of sagas and other Icelandic stories. If you are new to this world, I hope you will hang in there for the ride. I will try to provide some context. There will be suggestions for further reading.

I should also say that some of these poems stay fairly close to the original text or history. Others do not. For example, the shape-shifted queen in the first poem, *Egil*, is a swallow and also something of a literary critic. She picks right up on the technical innovations Egil is introducing in order to impress her husband. In the saga itself, Gunnhild indeed turns herself into a swallow, but her aim is simply to make bird noises and distract Egil. The poems take lots of other liberties. I hope readers familiar with these stories will enjoy these liberties, and forgive them, if necessary.

EGIL

VARIATIONS ON A SAGA

Egil Skallagrimsson is the hero, or some would say, the anti-hero of the thirteenth century *Egil's Saga*. Egil was a tenth century warrior and poet. He was a complicated and unsettling figure. Even by the standards of his time, he was considered to be erratic and overly violent. He was also their best poet. He once saved his life with a praise poem. His lament for his son is still celebrated.

Egil was unsettling physically, as well as in his behavior. He was swarthy, not one of the blond Vikings you could also find in his family. He had a disturbingly large head. His eyebrows were not normal. In one scene in the saga, after his brother has died in battle, his eyebrows do something very weird. A kind of facial shape-shifting. Speaking of shape-shifting, it was a tendency in his family. His family was also subject to premonitions.

Egil's Saga is a multi-generational story that takes place during a period of great upheaval in Norway. Harold Fairhair was consolidating his centralizing rule. Egil's family in Iceland have to work out their relationships with the rulers of Norway. Egil's adversary is Harold's son, Eric Bloodax. Eric's queen is Gunnhild, whom the sagas love. She appears in many of them. She is cold and vindictive, with sorcerers' ways. She is the shape-shifted swallow on Egil's branch in the first poem.

Three of the poems are based on *Egil's Lament*. Egil's son Bodvar drowned when he was a young man. Egil buried him and then he did not want to live any more. His daughter had to trick him back to life. She tricked him into taking nourishment, then told him he was the only one who could compose a proper lament for Bodvar. *Egil Is Baffled By Grief* and *Egil's Mouth* draw on phrases and images from the lament.

The sequence is not in strict chronological order, but I wanted to end with poems for both Gunnhild and Egil, aging. The Gunnhild poem actually comes from an episode in *Njal's Saga*. She is widowed. Eric is gone. The *Njal* author draws her with some poignancy. As for Egil, as you will see, he does not go gentle.

EGIL

Not all poets are sensitive and solitary.
Consider Egil Skallagrimsson,
Icelandic, tenth century.
The old sociopath was known
for the disproportions of his violence,
the strategic
deployment of his kennings,
his capacity for lament.
When necessary,
he could turn himself into metaphors.
A good poem
almost saved his life.
He stayed up all night,
made a better poem.
His enemy, the queen,
sat on a branch outside his window.
Her birdy,
judicious ear
caught
the technical innovation,
the Continental end rhymes,
and the praise,
and she knew her husband would fall for it.

EGIL SWIMS AWAY FROM EUROPE

Those were the days
in which Harold Fairhair
locked up Norway,
consolidated his hegemony,
combed down cowlicks.
Egil was unmanageable,
he was always starting up.
He could escape from anything.
He was a regular Houdini.
Once, his enemies tied him up,
so he could stew all night
over what they would do to him in the morning.
His large head schemed.
He threw the knots
into other-dimensioned space
until they loosened.
Then he escaped,
burned down the house.
Egil got tired of Europe.
He was an independent man.
He preferred the integrity of revenge
to law or social usage.
He dived into the water,
swam
until he heard the basaltic muttering,
the tectonic plates
where Europe bumps up against North America.

THE EYEBROWS

He had the family gift
of accurate
foreboding.
His brother's gone.
Egil's foreboding
could not save him.
Now he sits
in Athelstan's hall
and he will not drink.
His large head is bowed,
he is moving his sword
back and forth in its sheath,
but it's the eyebrows
that are the scariest.
They are dark and coarse,
as if sprung
from pelt,
and they are doing something
eyebrows
oughten't.

(continued)

They are migrating.
A hideous journey
from scalp
to chin,
then lurch,
reverse,
and back,
again.
Something unquiet
wants to be known.
It is his first
great grief poem.

BEAR

A bear has wandered into Egil's story.
It is not an avatar of Odin,
although Odin can be called Bear.
It is not the pelt
of a berserker,
although it is true
that Egil is angry.
No,
the bear seems to have come from a fairy tale
to frighten children.
The children are guarding sheep
and they tell Egil about the bear.
He is hiding in the woods.
They have been told to watch out for him.
They think Egil must not be very clever,
because he has not heard about the bear.
Egil is delighted by this.
He will use it in a ruse.
He has come for a child.
Not these children,
he will be friendly with them,
but for the king's son.
The king's son is ten years old.
He is sleeping.
Not even at the edges of his dream
does he hear the branches moving.

EGIL IS BAFFLED BY GRIEF

For Egil,
revenge
was the final stage of grief.
When his son
drowned,
he didn't know who to hurt.
He couldn't hurt the sea.
Odin
was beyond his reach.
So he stopped,
he simply
stopped.
His daughter
had to tell him
there was a poem
caught
in his throat.

EGIL IS SAVED BY A WOMAN

His boy, beached,
fetched up on shore.
Beyond
all bringing back.
He locked himself in his room.
He was determined to starve.
His daughter knocked at his door.
There was something in her mouth.
She told her father it was seaweed.
She needed to get that close to salt.
She'd brought some for him, too.
They maintained a silence.
It was thirsty work.
She asked him to send for water.
He tilted the horn,
knew he had been tricked.
Helpless,
his mouth
accepted milk,
and he wasn't sure
if he was still dying.
She asked him to make a poem.
She knew the early versions
would start to save him.
She was a poet
and a trickster,
like her old man.
The salt in the seaweed.
The milk in the horn.

EGIL'S MOUTH

He is intimate
and specific,
wants us to know
his mouth
from the inside,
before
words come,
when the throat
is stunned,
when the tongue
labors.
Earlier,
after violence,
he had improvised
a poem
about how his mouth
could bite.
This is different.

THORGERD

When Egil was twelve,
he was playing ball with his dad.
He was big for his age
and he started to win.
The men in that family
had a problem with nightfall.
They shape-shifted
into excessive strength
and rage.
Skallagrim put his hands on his son.
He wanted to hurt him.
Egil's old nurse
saw the commotion.
The saga says
she was a large woman,
strong as a man.
She rushed Skallagrim.
He chased her,
until she jumped into the sea.
He threw a rock,
that struck her,
and Thorgerd
went under.
She could not help
her kindness.
The rock
carried her
down.

ARINBJORN

He was a good friend.
He could read Egil's face
and tell
when he was working
on a poem.
He'd ask him
to come out with it,
and they'd discuss it,
discuss its merits and imperfections,
and whatever trouble
lay underneath.
He was not a poet,
but he gave sensible advice.
When Egil
got into deeper trouble
with the King,
he plotted the curve,
wrath
versus length,
thought he might escape
with twenty stanzas.
He maintained
good relations with the King,
Eric Bloodax.
He knew his flaws;
he looked for teachable moments.
He was surrounded by dangerous children,
whom he loved.
He was the only grown-up
in the story.

GUNNHILD

That winter,
she slept with him
in the upper room.
He was her scandal.
Her Icelander.
Her younger man.
People said,
Gunnhild
gets what she wants,
but this was not
entirely true.
There was something
this man
withheld.
A place
she could not
enter.
This worried her,
but it held her
steady.
Her contempt,
which had such a long
history
with Eric,
learned limits.
It was as close
to love
as she would come,
and it held,
for a season.

Egil Faces The Challenges Of Aging

Egil is going blind
and it pisses him off.
Even the servants tell him
he is old and in the way.
They tell him to move away
from the fire.
He is interrupting their work.
Too far from the hearth,
he inventories
what's left.
Fury
and his accumulated treasure.
He will bring it
to the Althing,
strew it all around,
and laugh,
when everyone acts foolish.
It will be his last contempt poem.
His son-in-law won't let him.
Egil doesn't like to be balked.
He goes out one night,
takes two servants,
and buries the treasure.
The servants don't come back.
He is big again.

SNORRI

A Lament

Snorri Sturluson was a thirteenth century writer, chieftain, and politician. For English speakers, Snorri's name can sound like a diminutive. It was not, but I think we are right to hear a child. A brilliant child. A playful child. A child who could be greedy.

When Snorri was three years old, his life changed utterly. During a rough patch in a lawsuit, a woman came at Snorri's father with a knife. She said she wanted to make him like his hero, Odin, who had famously sacrificed an eye for wisdom. Iceland was Christian by then, but people would have gotten the reference.

A settlement was brokered. Snorri became part of the settlement. He would be fostered by Jon Loftsson, the most influential man in Iceland. He would be raised at Oddi, a center of learning. Jon Loftsson was related to the kings of Norway. For Snorri, learning, power, and the allure of royalty would always be enmeshed.

Snorri fell in love with the old poetry of the Norse skaldic tradition. This poetry had been hard to follow, even when it had been composed, due to its complicated, often glancing allusions to Norse mythology. As the old pagan stories faded, the poetry became even harder to follow.

In his *Edda*, Snorri tried to reclaim the old stories and the old poetic craft. He told his own versions of the stories. He passed on technical knowledge of kennings and meters.

The *Edda* was intended for the education of the rulers of Norway and, of course, for Snorri's self-promotion. but the impact of the *Edda* has been far broader. It is through Snorri, mainly, that the old stories of Norse mythology have come down to us. He preserved them. He shaped them and in some ways he recreated them.

Snorri is at his best on the page. When we read the *Edda*, we are in good hands. We consent to be dazzled by him. We want his guile, his playful brilliance, his subtle intelligence. Many of his contemporaries were less charmed by him. Snorri was greedy. There was a coldness to him. His alliances did not hold. He made dangerous missteps in his long dance with the rulers of Norway.

His enemies broke into his home at Reykholt in 1241. Snorri hid, but he knew he could not escape.

I give Egil the last poem in the sequence. He was one of Snorri's ancestors, on his mother's side. He had the gift of accurate foreboding and he was good with laments.

SNORRI LEARNS THE WORLD IS WIDE

Snorri's journey toward wisdom
began
when a woman offered to cut away
his father's eye,
a gesture
toward an old story.
His father kept the eye,
traded the threat
for a transaction.
His youngest son,
brokered
into a world of influence and learning.
Snorri was three years old.
He left his father's home.
He would learn to love libraries,
and to scheme east,
across the water.
He would learn the world is wide
and its coasts,
deeply indented.

THE OLD POEMS

He loves
the difficult
tradition
of the old poems.
He loves
their stealth
and indirection.
A lost honey
enters his blood.

EDDA

He demotes them,
a little.
He is telling their stories
in Christian Iceland.
He euhemerizes,
great word,
rationalizes,
if you can call it that,
mapping the old gods
onto Troy.
Then he settles down
into his serious
play.
Stories
within stories,
in a hall
that vanishes.

Snorri Loses Sleep

Something
has gotten into
Snorri's horse.
His horse has developed
a sixth gait,
a subtle alteration
in timing.
It is more subtle than Snorri.
He cannot follow it,
cannot feel his way
into the altered hitch
and swing.
It is a rogue meter,
one of the old skaldic meters
he disturbed
when he was showing off
for the Norwegians.
He is deeply unsettled.
It is a warning.
He has overreached himself,
again.

SNORRI, CORNERED

He wasn't a bit like Yeats,
but I imagine him
at the end,
alone
with his heart,
saying goodbye
to his circus animals,
all of his beautiful
circus animals.
Entire mythologies.
Ragnarok
in the final room.
A finished man
among his enemies.

Snorri's Last Words

enter collective
memory
as Don't Cut! Don't Cut!
His enemies
broke into his story,
told it their own way.

EGIL'S LAMENT

They're generations
apart,
but already
it feels
as if something
has been torn.
He extends his lament,
with the sad prescience
of his kin,
toward Snorri,
toward Reykholt,
where Snorri
has fallen
without serviceable words.

THE MEAD OF POETRY

In the *Edda*, Snorri tells the story of the Mead of Poetry, how gods and humans received the gift of poetic inspiration.

Snorri's story is wonderfully episodic. It involves violence, conniving, and several different kinds of body fluids.

In the central episode, Odin tracks the mead to a cavern guarded by Gunnlod, a giant's daughter. They negotiate. He agrees to spend three nights with her, in exchange for three sips of the Mead of Poetry. Of course, he cheats and escapes with all of the mead.

The first poem is a celebration of the unruliness, the commotion of Snorri's account. The second poem is a counter-story. It re-imagines the three nights with the giantess.

COMMOTION

There's a certain misogyny
here,
(how large
women are,
how demanding)
but I think,
on balance,
Snorri gets it right
about Odin's three nights
with the giantess.
How poetry
is not only
a fine ferment,
but also
carries with it
a history
of commotion,
skirmish,
the ogre's bed.
How even
in its origin story,
the poet
is formed
from spittle,
the honey
mixed with blood.

GUNNLOD

He sat
in the crook of her arm,
felt warmed
by something almost geothermal.
He loved the sound of her voice.
He loved the chambered resonance
of her vowels.
Her enormous brain
held fold upon fold
of poetry.
Riddles, boasts, incantations.
Praise poetry.
Opaque poetry.
Poetry
translucent as amber.
She knew the human heart,
and because she was a giant,
she knew about things
that were elemental.
She knew the voice of frost.
She knew the vulnerability of ice
as it remembers water.
She was fleshy
and archival.
Canonical
and non-canonical.
He sat up with her
for three nights.
The old god,
delighted.

Suggestions For Further Reading

If you want to read *Egil's Saga* or Snorri's *Edda*, you will have many choices. I don't pretend to be an expert on translations or editions. A good choice for *Egil's Saga* would be the Penguin Classics edition, translated by Hermann Pálsson, with Paul Edwards. For Snorri's *Edda*, people seem to think highly of the translation by Anthony Faulkes. You can find this in an Everyman's Library edition. Snorri's *Edda* is also called the *Prose Edda* or the *Younger Edda*. Faulkes calls his translation simply *Edda*. The *Poetic*, or *Elder Edda* is a collection of the older Norse poetry that Snorri loved. It is a wonderful source of the old stories. If you want to read more by Snorri, you can look for *Heimskringla*, his massive account of the history of the kings of Norway.

Heimskringla can be translated as the orb or circle of the earth. The title is taken from the opening lines. Snorri may have been writing about Norway, but he was going to start out with the whole world.

For a thoughtful article on Egil, with a wonderful account of the scene between Egil and his daughter, I would recommend *Egil Skallagrimsson and the Viking Ideal*, by Professor Christina von Nolcken. The article is available online, through the University of Chicago's *Fathom Archive*.

For a very expressive biography of Snorri, I would recommend *Song of the Vikings: Snorri and the Making of Norse Myths*, by Nancy Marie Brown. You will find the man in all his colors. Her most recent book, *Ivory Vikings*, provides more context for the intellectual and artistic life at Oddi, where Snorri was raised.

ACKNOWLEDGMENTS

Many of these poems were published as micro-chapbooks by the Origami Poems Project.

Thanks to editors Lynnie Gobeille and Jan Keogh for being open to these stories.

Do yourself a favor. Check out the Origami Poems Project online.

Gunnlod was heard, in a somewhat different form, on WRNI, the Rhode Island affiliate of National Public Radio, as part of their *This I Believe* series. The piece, with an accompanying essay, was called *The Power of Poetry*.

About the Author

Nancy Jasper is a clinical social worker. She considers herself part of the great English Major diaspora. She has published five micro-chapbooks with the Origami Poems Project.

In 2015, the OPP nominated her for a Pushcart Prize. Her poems have also appeared in *Leviathan*, *Gávea-Brown*, *The Wrack Line*, and the anthology, *Missing Providence*.

Nancy's poems and essays have been heard on WRNI, the Rhode Island affiliate of National Public Radio, as part of their *This I Believe* series.

Nancy has been a featured reader at a range of venues. She loves sharing her Icelandic poems with new audiences.